WHO WOULD WIN?®

LOBSTER

VS.

CRAB

BY
JERRY PALLOTTA

ILLUSTRATED BY
ROB BOLSTER

Scholastic Inc.

The publisher would like to thank the following for their
kind permission to use their photographs in this book:

Page 13 top-right image: flySnow / Thinkstock; bottom-right image: Pigprox / Shutterstock;
page 17 crab pot: NOAA Central Library Historical Fisheries Collection;
page 20 top image: Carol Perry Davis; bottom image: Dorset Media Service / Alamy;
page 21 bottom image: Shari Romar; page 25 top image: Millard H. Sharp / Science Source.

To Bob, Betsy, and especially Christopher Detwiler.
— J.P.
To Charlie, Eddie, Bobby D., and Teddy.
— R.B.

ISBN 978-0-545-68121-6

18 17 16 15 14 13

17 18 19/0

Printed in the U.S.A.
First printing, December 2014

40

What if a lobster and a crab bumped into each other. What if they had a fight? Who do you think would win?

WHICH LOBSTER?

Which lobster should fight the crab?

SPINY LOBSTER

Spiny lobster from the Caribbean? Sorry, you are spiky, but have no claws.

PINK SPOTTED PRAWN

Pink spotted prawn? No way! You are a shrimp, not a lobster.

Shovel-nosed lobster? Nope, you are strange looking. Go dig up a clam!

SHOVEL-NOSED LOBSTER

American lobster? Perfect! Two claws.

AMERICAN LOBSTER

WHICH CRAB?

Which crab should fight the lobster?

DUNGENESS CRAB

Dungeness crab? No! It is famous in San Francisco and on the West Coast. Its shell is rubbery.

ALASKAN KING CRAB

Alaskan king crab? No! You have only six legs. You are popular in restaurants all over the world.

> **FACT**
> *Crabs have eight legs and two claws.*

HORSESHOE CRAB

Horseshoe crab? No! You are not even a crab. You look prehistoric!

BLUE CRAB

Blue crab? Yes, you are one of the best-known crabs in the world. And maybe the best tasting.

MEET THE LOBSTER

The American lobster's scientific name is *Homarus americanus*. It lives off America's northeast and Canada's east coasts.

FACT
Lobsters have a muscular tail.

FACT
Lobsters are in an animal family called crustaceans.

WILD FACT
A lobster's teeth are in its stomach.

The largest lobster was about three feet long and weighed 44 pounds.

MEET THE BLUE CRAB

This is a blue crab. It is the most popular crab in the world. Its scientific name is *Callinectes sapidus*, which means "beautiful savory swimmer."

DEFINITION
Savory means pleasant or agreeable in taste or smell.

BITE FACT
A blue crab can't bite with its mouth. A grinding mill inside its body chews its food.

DID YOU KNOW?
Blue crabs are known as "swimming crabs."

DID YOU KNOW?
A blue crab does not have a tail.

The largest blue crab was about one foot wide and weighed a little more than one pound.

WHERE DO LOBSTERS LIVE?

American lobsters live from North Carolina's coastline up to Canada's east coast. Lobsters can be found in shallow water close to shore and also in deep water miles out.

CANADA

UNITED STATES

Range of the American lobster

WHERE DO CRABS LIVE?

Blue crabs are most often found from the south shore of Cape Cod in Massachusetts all the way down to the Texas-Mexico border. Chesapeake Bay is one of the most famous places for blue crabs.

FACT
Chesapeake Bay is an estuary. An estuary is where the ocean meets a river.

U.S.A.

Range of the blue crab in the U.S.

BONUS FACT
More than 150 rivers and streams empty into the Chesapeake Bay.

DID YOU KNOW?
Blue crabs love shallow, brackish water.

DEFINITION
Brackish water is part salt and part freshwater.

MEXICO

9

LOBSTER PARTS

The lobster's head and thorax is one piece. It's called a *cephalothorax*. A lobster has eight legs, just like a spider and a scorpion.

SCISSOR CLAW

FACT
The lobster feeds itself with its four front legs.

CRUSHER CLAW

ANTENNAE

MOUTH

EYE

FEEDING LEGS

CEPHALOTHORAX

KNUCKLE

LEGS

SPEED LIMIT

TAIL FACT
The American lobster has five flaps at the end of its tail.

TAIL

On land, lobsters cannot walk well. The front two legs on each side have pincers on them.

CRAB ANATOMY

The blue crab's body is one piece. Its shell is called a *carapace*.

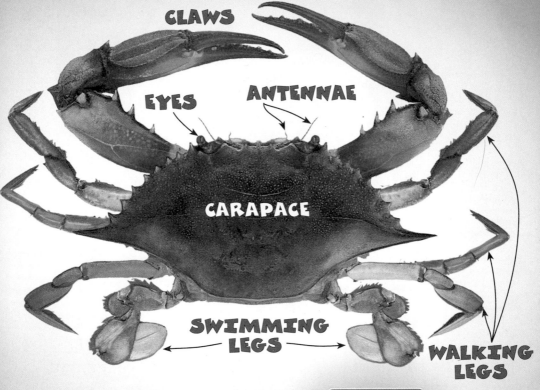

CLAWS

EYES

ANTENNAE

CARAPACE

SWIMMING LEGS

WALKING LEGS

SPEED LIMIT 10

Blue crabs can swim well, and they're also great runners. They can run fast on land.

BOY

The crusher claw of a male lobster is bigger and wider than a female crusher claw. The flaps under the tail are called swimmerettes.

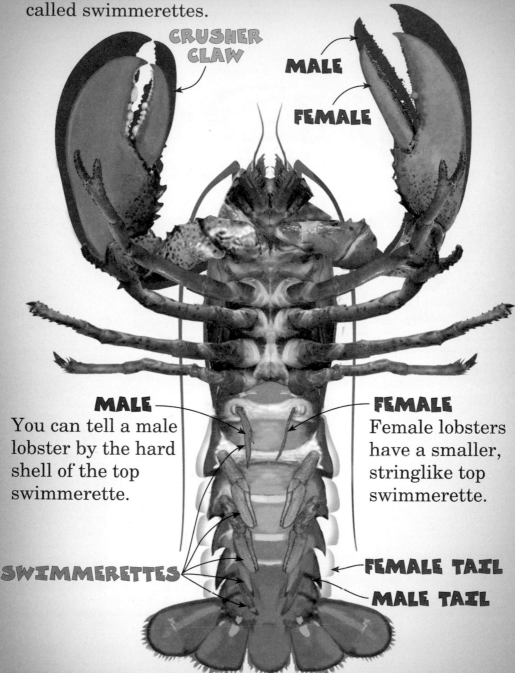

CRUSHER CLAW

MALE

FEMALE

MALE
You can tell a male lobster by the hard shell of the top swimmerette.

FEMALE
Female lobsters have a smaller, stringlike top swimmerette.

SWIMMERETTES

FEMALE TAIL

MALE TAIL

Female lobster tails are wider than male lobster tails.

OR GIRL!

Crabs have a flap between their eight legs that is called an apron or a leaf. The girls' leaf is shaped like the Capitol Dome. Girl blue crabs also have red tips on their claws. They look like painted fingernails.

CAPITOL DOME

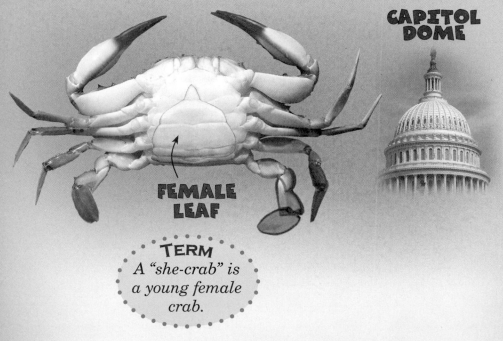

FEMALE LEAF

TERM
A "she-crab" is a young female crab.

Boy blue crabs have a skinny leaf. Some say it is shaped like the Washington Monument.

WASHINGTON MONUMENT

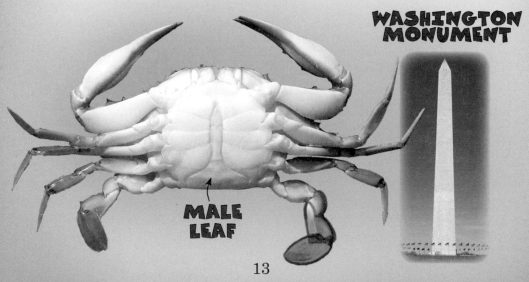

MALE LEAF

LOBSTER CLAWS

The two claws of a lobster are different. The crusher claw is dull and the scissor claw is sharp.

CRUSHER CLAW

The crusher claw is slower and stronger, and usually wider. The scissor claw is quicker and skinnier.

DID YOU KNOW?
Some kids call them a cruncher claw and a ripper claw. Other kids call them a smasher claw and a slasher claw.

SCISSOR CLAW

Either claw could be on the right or the left.

CRAB PINCERS

Can you call them claws or pincers?
Both words are correct.

CLAW TYPE
*Blue crab claws are
not specialized.*

FACT
*The claws of a blue crab are similar. Each claw
is a mirror image of the other claw.*

QUESTION?
*Is this blue crab
male or female?*

ANSWER
*The clues you'll need
are on page 13.*

LOBSTER BAIT

Most lobsters are caught by traps. Traps are baited with fish heads, fish guts, and fish bones.

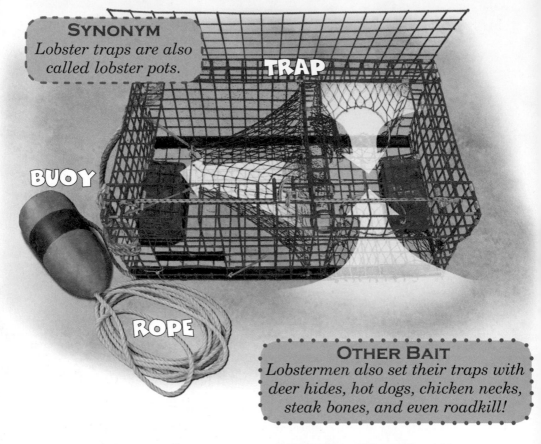

TRAP

BUOY

ROPE

OTHER BAIT
Lobstermen also set their traps with deer hides, hot dogs, chicken necks, steak bones, and even roadkill!

BUOY COLOR?

A buoy is a marker that floats on top of the water. Lobstermen can tell their gear by the colors of the buoy.

QUESTION?
If you were a lobsterman or lobsterwoman, what colors would your buoy be?

CATCH A CRAB

Blue crabs are caught by crab pots, trotlines, and by a dip net.

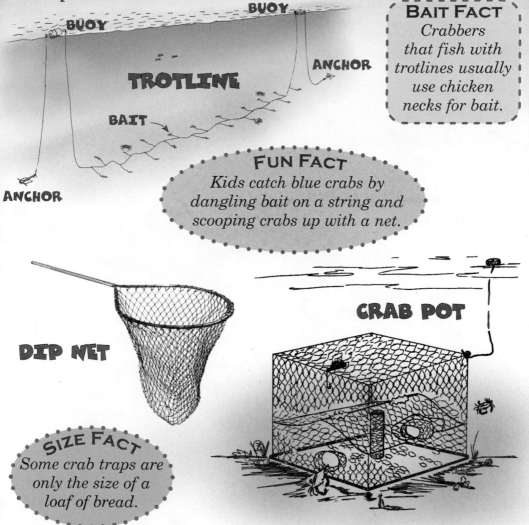

BUOY

BUOY

ANCHOR

TROTLINE

BAIT

ANCHOR

BAIT FACT
Crabbers that fish with trotlines usually use chicken necks for bait.

FUN FACT
Kids catch blue crabs by dangling bait on a string and scooping crabs up with a net.

DIP NET

CRAB POT

SIZE FACT
Some crab traps are only the size of a loaf of bread.

Crabs love fresh bait. Chicken, fish, steak, or any meat works well.

CHICKEN

FISH

STEAK

EXOSKELETON

Lobsters have an exoskeleton, which is a hard shell on the outside of their bodies. To grow larger, lobsters have to climb out of their shells and then grow a larger shell. This is called molting.

■ **OLD EXOSKELETON**

■ **MOLTING SOFT SHELL LOBSTER**

HARDSHELL
A lobster with a hard shell.

FACT
The younger a lobster is, the more it molts.

GROSS FACT
After molting, a lobster eats its old shell.

SOFT SHELL
A recently molted lobster whose shell is delicate.

MOLTING

Crabs also have an exoskeleton and molt to grow larger.

DID YOU KNOW?
A *"peeler"* is a crab about to shed its shell.

DEFINITION
A *"hardshell"* is a crab that is not molting and has a hard shell.

■ **OLD EXOSKELETON**

■ **MOLTING SOFT SHELL CRAB**

SOFT FACT
A *"soft shell"* is a crab that has just shed its shell.

FACT
A crustacean that molts is vulnerable to predators while in a soft state.

EGGER

A female lobster with eggs is called an egger or a seeder. She carries the eggs, which are dark green, under her tail attached to her body and swimmerettes.

DID YOU KNOW?
Out of 50,000 eggs, it is estimated that only two grow up to be as large as their mother.

The eggs turn light orange and hatch. The mom lobster carries between 3,000 and 75,000 eggs.

TASTY FACT
One day after hatching, about half the eggs get eaten by fish and other predators.

BABY LOBSTER

SPONGER

A sponger is a female crab with eggs. The crab below is a female blue crab whose leaf is full of eggs.

EGGS

Scientists think there are up to two million eggs in a large blue crab.

BABY BLUE CRAB

LOBSTER EYES

Lobsters can't see well. They have antennae that sense vibrations in the water. They have a great sense of smell.

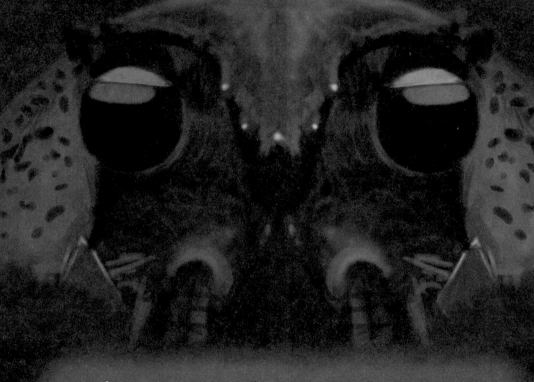

LOBSTER TERMS

KEEPER
A lobster large enough to legally keep.

V-NOTCH TAIL
A female lobster that has been notched by the Department of Fisheries cannot be kept.

CHICKEN LOBSTER
A keeper lobster that weighs under 1 pound.

CULL
A lobster with only one claw.

CRAB EYES

Crabs can't see well. They have a great sense of smell and their antennae can sense motion.

CRAB VOCABULARY

SOOK
A mature female blue crab.

JIMMY
A male blue crab.

WEAPONS

Lobsters have spikes all over their shells. They are armored and ready for battle.

Spikes on the nose.

Spikes on the tail.

Spikes on the knuckles.

FACT
A lobster can curl its tail and cut your fingers or hand.

DEFENSIVE FACT
Lobsters use their claws to defend themselves against fish and other creatures.

MEASURING

QUESTION?
How do you measure a lobster?

ANSWER
With a lobster gauge.

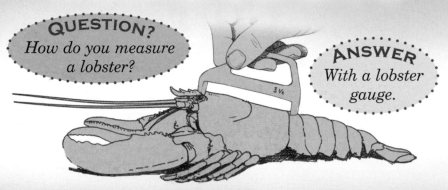

Measure from the eye socket to the end of its head. In most states, the head must be 3-¼ inches long to be a keeper.

ARMOR

A crab has sharp points around its body. Take a good look at a blue crab. Predators can't easily swallow it.

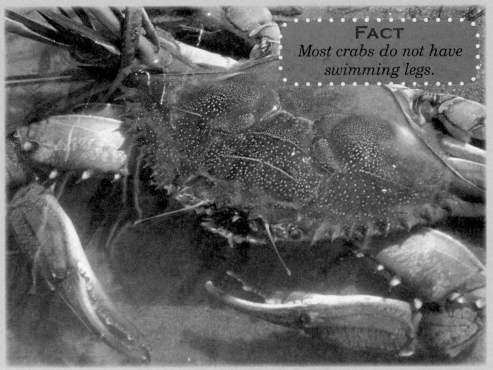

FACT
Most crabs do not have swimming legs.

GAUGE

QUESTION?
How do you measure a blue crab?

ANSWER
With a crab gauge.

Measure a crab from point to point, from side to side. In most states, a crab must be at least five inches long to be a keeper.

ARE YOU HUNGRY?

Someone once said, "Everything tastes like chicken, but nothing tastes as good as lobster."

BIG JOE'S LOBSTER
TODAY'S SPECIALS

Boiled lobster
Baked stuffed lobster
Lobster thermidor
Lobster bisque
Lobster taco
Lobster newburg
Lobster macaroni and cheese

EAT BEFORE THE FIGHT

Other people say blue crab is the greatest food on earth.

The lobster wants to be left alone. It climbs into a crevice. The crab wants to be left alone, too. It burrows into some mud.

They both get hungry. The crab walks around, looking for food. It stumbles upon the lobster. The crab tries to take a bite.

Whoosh! The lobster flaps its tail and gets away.
The crab runs after it. Whoosh! Another flap of its tail,
and the lobster gets away. But the lobster is hungry. It
walks claws-first at the crab.

The crab flaps its paddle-shaped legs and swims over
to the lobster. The lobster is patient. When the crab
gets close, the lobster attacks.

The lobster's quick scissor claw grabs the crab by one of its claws. The lobster's crusher claw swings over and *crack*! The lobster damages the crab's claw.

The lobster grabs a couple of legs. Now the crab can't run away. The lobster and the crab fight back and forth. The crab's claws are not strong enough to hurt the lobster.

The lobster moves its crusher claw and bites a chunk off the crab's face.

The crab fills with water from the hole in its shell. This is fatal. The crab slowly stops moving.

The lobster agrees with people. Crabs are delicious.

WHO HAS THE ADVANTAGE?
CHECKLIST

LOBSTER   BLUE CRAB

LOBSTER		BLUE CRAB
☐	Size	☐
☐	Shell	☐
☐	Claws	☐
☐	Legs	☐
☐	Teeth	☐
☐	Speed	☐
☐	Tail	☐

Author note: This is one way the fight might have ended.
How would you write the ending?